Ice Cream

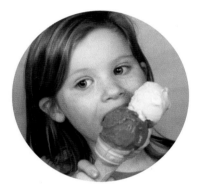

Written by Frances Lee

Photography by Michael Curtain

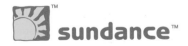
sundance™

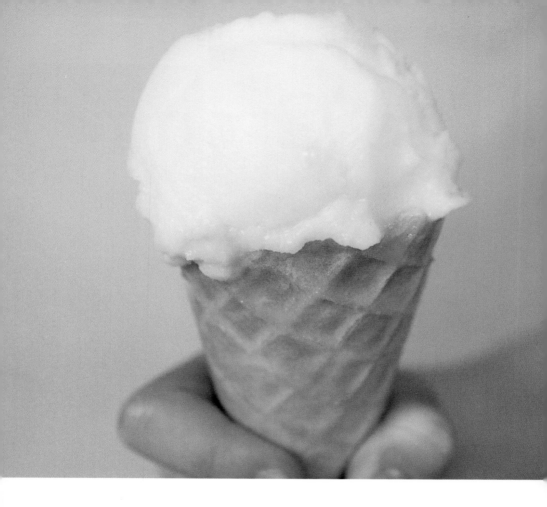

This is white ice cream.

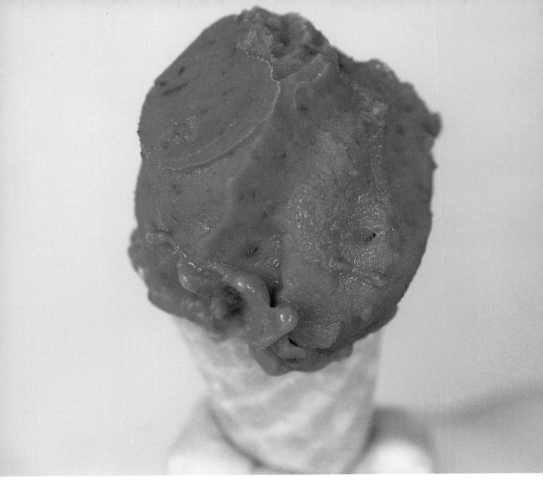

This is red ice cream.

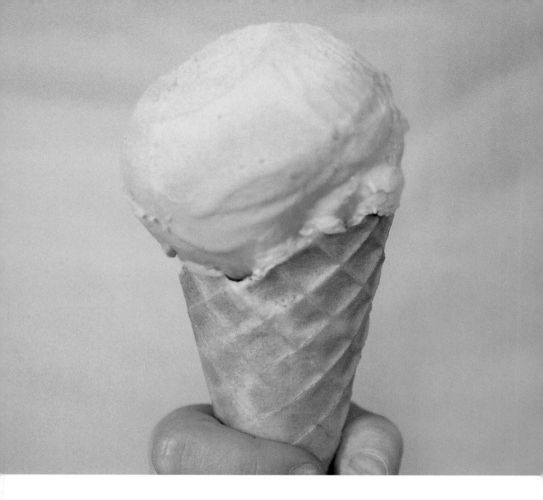

This is green ice cream.

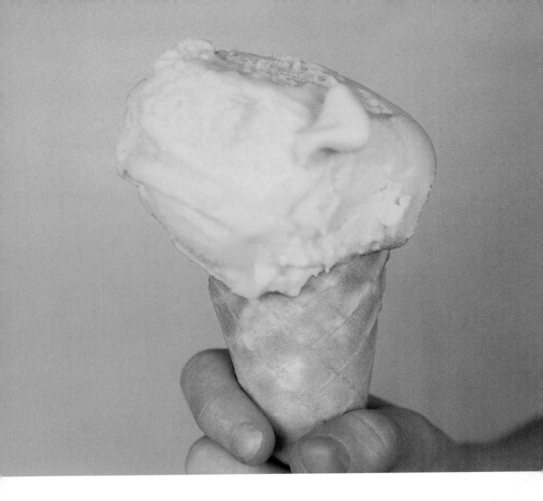

This is yellow ice cream.

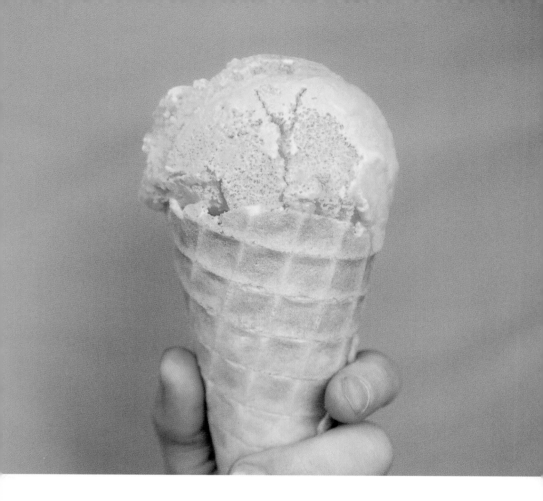

This is orange ice cream.

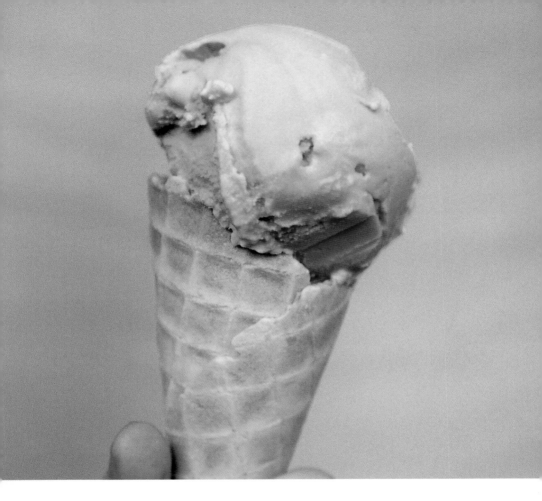

This is blue ice cream.

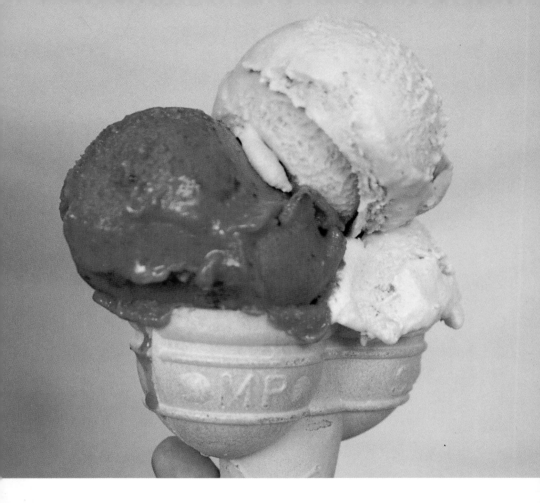

This is my ice cream!